Learning about Cats

THE
ORIENTAL CAT

by Joanne Mattern

Consultant:
Lynn Miller
Secretary, Oriental Shorthairs of America
Author, *The Guide to Owning an
Oriental Shorthair Cat*

CAPSTONE
HIGH-INTEREST
BOOKS

an imprint of Capstone Press
Mankato, Minnesota

Capstone High-Interest Books are published by Capstone Press
151 Good Counsel Drive, P.O. Box 669, Mankato, Minnesota 56002
http://www.capstone-press.com

Library of Congress Cataloging-in-Publication Data
Mattern, Joanne, 1963–
    The Oriental cat/by Joanne Mattern.
    p. cm.—(Learning about cats)
    Includes bibliographical references (p. 45) and index.
    Summary: Discusses the history, development, habits, and care of Oriental cats.
    ISBN 0-7368-1303-9 (hardcover)
    1. Oriental shorthair cat—Juvenile literature. 2. Oriental longhair cat—Juvenile
literature. [1. Oriental shorthair cat. 2. Oriental longhair cat. 3. Cats.] I. Title.
II. Series.
SF449.O73 M38 2003
636.8'2—dc21   2001007718

Editorial Credits
Angela Kaelberer, editor; Karen Risch, product planning editor; Linda Clavel,
    series designer and illustrator; Gene Bentdahl, book designer; Jo Miller,
    photo researcher

Photo Credits
Chanan Photography, 10, 13, 27, 36
Karen Hudson, 9, 23
Larry Johnson, 24, 32
Lynn Miller, 35
Nancy M. McCallum, 16, 19, 20, 28, 31
Photo by Mark McCullough, cover, 4, 6, 14, 40–41
www.ronkimballstock.com, 39

1 2 3 4 5 6 07 06 05 04 03 02

Table of Contents

Quick Facts about the Oriental

Description

Size: Orientals are medium-sized cats.

Weight: A full-grown Oriental weighs between 5 and 11 pounds (2.3 and 5 kilograms).

Physical features: The Oriental is a slim cat with a long tail. Orientals can be either shorthaired or longhaired. Oriental Shorthairs have short, fine fur. Oriental Longhairs have long, silky fur.

Color:	The coats of Oriental cats can be one of more than 300 colors and color patterns.

Development

Place of origin:	The Oriental Shorthair breed began in Great Britain. Breeders in the United States and Great Britain began the Oriental Longhair breed.
History of breed:	In the 1950s, breeders in Great Britain bred Siamese cats to cats of other breeds to create the Oriental Shorthair. Oriental Longhairs did not appear until the 1980s. They resulted from mating Orientals with longhaired cats of other breeds.
Numbers:	In 2001, there were 988 Oriental cats registered in North America with the Cat Fanciers' Association (CFA). Owners who register their Orientals list the cats' breeding records with an official club. The CFA is the largest organization of cat breeders in North America. The International Cat Association (TICA) and the American Cat Fanciers Association (ACFA) are other popular North American cat associations.

Chapter 1

The Oriental Cat

The Oriental is a curious, friendly, and playful breed. These slender, graceful cats can demand a great deal of attention from their owners. But many people enjoy the cats' active personalities.

Appearance

The Oriental cat has a long, thin body. Some people say the cat's body is shaped like a tube. People sometimes compare Orientals to Greyhounds. Like the Greyhound, the Oriental has a long, narrow body and a long, thin tail.

Male Oriental cats usually weigh 7 to 11 pounds (3.1 to 5 kilograms). Females are smaller. They usually weigh 5 to 9 pounds (2.3 to 4 kilograms).

The Oriental cat has a long, thin body.

Orientals can be either shorthaired or longhaired. An Oriental Shorthair's fur is fine and smooth. Oriental Longhairs have softer, silkier fur than Oriental Shorthairs do. An Oriental's fur lies close to its body.

Orientals' coats can be one of more than 300 colors or color patterns. Orientals of most colors and patterns can compete in cat shows.

Personality

Orientals are active cats. They seem to like being the center of attention. Orientals often try to be involved in all of their owners' activities.

Like Siamese cats, most Orientals have loud meows. They meow often to let their owners know their wants and needs.

Orientals' long, slender back legs allow them to climb and jump easily. Owners often find their Orientals sitting on top of refrigerators, bookcases, windows, and doors.

Orientals are playful. They may pick up and play with objects such as pens, gloves, and

Most Orientals have loud meows.

watches. Some cat breeds are playful only as kittens. But Orientals remain playful as adults.

Orientals make good family pets. They usually get along well with children. They also do well in homes that have other cats or dogs. These cats do not seem to enjoy being alone.

Chapter 2

Development of the Breed

The Oriental Shorthair breed began in Great Britain about 50 years ago. The Oriental Longhair breed began about 30 years later in Great Britain and the United States. Both types were developed through careful breeding.

The First Orientals

The first Oriental cats were bred in Great Britain during the 1950s. Breeders wanted a cat that had a long, narrow body like a Siamese cat. But they wanted the cat to have different colors and patterns than the Siamese. Siamese cats have light-colored coats with darker fur on their face, ears, paws, and tail. These darker areas are called points.

An Oriental cat's long, narrow body is similar to that of a Siamese cat.

People bred Siamese cats to Persians, Korats, British Shorthairs, Russian Blues, and Abyssinians. These matings led to a large variety of colors and patterns.

In Great Britain, the resulting cats first had several names. Brown solid-colored cats were called Havanas. Cats with solid-colored fur of another color were called Foreigns. Cats with markings were called Maus. By the 1970s, cats of these breeds were known as Oriental Shorthairs.

In 1972, two U.S. breeders of Siamese cats visited Great Britain and saw Oriental Shorthairs. The breeders' names were Peter and Vicky Markstein. The Marksteins helped bring several Oriental Shorthairs to the United States. These cats began the Oriental Shorthair breed in North America.

In 1977, the Cat Fanciers' Association (CFA) accepted the Oriental Shorthair for competition. The Oriental Shorthair soon became one of the CFA's most popular breeds.

Oriental Longhairs

A litter of Oriental Shorthairs can sometimes include one or more longhaired kittens. In the

Oriental Longhairs (right) have longer, silkier fur than Oriental Shorthairs (left) do.

1980s, several breeders in Great Britain and the United States began trying to breed longhaired Orientals. These breeders mated Oriental Shorthairs with longhaired cats. The resulting kittens looked like Oriental Shorthairs. But they had longer, silkier fur than Oriental Shorthairs do.

Oriental Longhairs' coats are different than those of other longhaired cats. Most longhaired

cats have a double coat. Their undercoat is thick and plush. Their outer coat is long and silky. Oriental Longhairs do not have a double coat. For this reason, their fur does not look as long or thick as that of other longhaired cats. Their fur appears longest on the tail.

Today, Oriental Longhairs can compete in most cat shows. In 1985, The International Cat Association (TICA) accepted Oriental Longhairs for competition. The CFA accepted the breed in 1995.

An Oriental Longhair's fur appears longest on its tail.

Chapter 3

Today's Oriental

Today, the Oriental breed is gaining popularity in North America. People enjoy this cat's active, friendly personality and its interesting appearance.

Breed Standard

Cat show officials look for several physical features when they judge an Oriental cat. These features are called the breed standard.

An Oriental cat that meets the breed standard is long, slim, and muscular. Its neck is long and slender. The shoulders are narrow. The legs are long and slim. The back legs are a little longer than the front legs.

An ideal Oriental cat's head is shaped like a wedge. It looks like an upside-down triangle.

An Oriental cat that meets the breed standard is long, slim, and muscular.

The nose is long and straight. The ears are large, wide, and pointed.

Nearly all Oriental cats have green eyes. White Orientals may have green eyes, blue eyes, or one eye of each color.

All Orientals should have long tails. An Oriental Shorthair has a long, thin tail that looks like a whip. An Oriental Longhair's tail should spread out like a long, fluffy feather.

An Oriental Shorthair's coat is short and fine. The fur should lie close to the cat's body. Oriental Longhairs should have medium-length, silky hair. The fur should be fine and have no plush inner layer.

Color

Orientals' coats have a great variety of colors and color patterns. More than 300 combinations of colors and patterns are possible. Common solid colors are black, white, chestnut, cinnamon, blue, red, and lavender. Chestnut and cinnamon are shades of brown. Blue is a shade of gray. Red is a shade of orange. Lavender is a pink-gray color.

Other color patterns include tabby, tortoiseshell, bi-color, pointed, shaded, and

Solid and tabby are common Oriental color patterns.

smoke. Tabby Orientals have striped, swirled, spotted, or ticked markings. Orientals with ticked coats have light and dark bands of color on each hair. Tortoiseshells' coats are a mixture of red and black fur. Bi-color coats have patches of white and one other color or pattern. Shaded Orientals have silver coats with colored tips at the end of each hair. Smoke Orientals have coats that appear to be one solid color. But each hair on a smoke Oriental is silver at the base.

Chapter 4

Owning an Oriental

People who want an Oriental cat can find one in several ways. Some people buy Orientals from breeders or pet stores. Other people adopt Orientals from animal shelters or breed rescue organizations.

Animal shelters and breed rescue organizations usually charge much less for Orientals than breeders do. Breeders often charge several hundred dollars for an Oriental kitten. But breeders often sell retired show cats for less money than kittens would cost.

Breeders

People who want a show-quality Oriental should buy one from a good breeder. Most breeders make sure their cats are healthy and

People who want a show-quality Oriental should buy one from a good breeder.

meet the breed standard. Breeders usually own one or both of the kittens' parents. Buyers often can see the kittens' parents. The buyers then can see how the kittens may look and act when grown.

Many Oriental cat breeders live in the United States and Canada. People often can meet breeders and see their cats at cat shows. Some Oriental breeders advertise in cat magazines or have their own Internet sites.

Before buying a cat, people should check the breeders' references. They can talk to people who have bought cats from the breeders. Buyers also should get the medical histories of the breeders' cats.

Animal Shelters

An animal shelter can be an inexpensive place to find a pet. Animal shelters try to find new homes for unwanted pets.

Few Orientals are available at shelters. Shelters often have mixed-breed pets instead of purebred cats such as the Oriental. But people who want to adopt an Oriental can

People who buy kittens from breeders often can meet the kittens' parents.

contact a shelter. They can ask shelter workers to contact them if an Oriental is brought to the shelter.

People who adopt pets from shelters may save the animals' lives. Many more animals are brought to shelters than there are people available to adopt them. Animals that are not adopted often are euthanized. Shelter

Orientals that can compete at cat shows are seldom available from animal shelters.

workers euthanize animals by injecting them with substances that stop their breathing or heartbeat.

Most animal shelters are less expensive than pet stores or breeders. They usually charge people only a small fee to adopt a pet. Local veterinarians often provide discounts on medical services for shelter animals.

Animal shelters may not be a good choice for everyone. Some people want to adopt an Oriental cat to breed or show. Pets adopted from a shelter seldom have registration papers. These papers list the pet's breeder and parents. Cats need these papers to compete in cat shows. Shelter workers may not have information about the animals' parents, health, or behavior. Some of these cats may have medical or behavioral problems.

Despite these facts, many good pets are available at animal shelters. Shelter Orientals may be a good choice for owners who do not plan to breed or show their cats.

Breed Rescue Organizations

People who want a purebred Oriental cat may want to contact a breed rescue organization. Rescue organizations are similar to animal shelters in many ways. But they usually only work with one or two cat breeds. They rarely euthanize the cats. They keep the cats until they find good homes for them.

A rescue organization can have some advantages over breeders and animal shelters. Orientals from rescue organizations usually are less expensive than those from breeders. Some rescue organizations even have Oriental cats with registration papers.

People can find information about rescue organizations in several ways. These organizations often have Internet sites. They also may advertise in magazines or newspapers. Animal shelter workers also may know of local rescue organizations.

Pet Stores

Oriental cats rarely are found at pet stores. But store workers may be able to find an Oriental from a local breeder.

Many pet stores are clean and sell healthy pets. But some stores do not take proper care of their animals. People should visit the pet store before they buy a pet. Buyers should ask employees where the store gets its pets. They

Registered Orientals may be available from rescue organizations.

should make sure the pets look healthy and alert. The pets should be housed in large, clean cages. They should have plenty of food, toys, and fresh water. A veterinarian should have recently checked the pets' health. The pets' medical records also should be available to buyers.

Chapter 5

Caring for an Oriental

The Oriental is a strong, healthy breed. With good care, Orientals can live 15 to 20 years or longer.

Indoor Cat Care

Owners can help their Orientals live long, healthy lives by keeping them inside. Orientals' curious personalities could put them in many dangerous situations outdoors. Outdoor cats are more likely to get diseases from other animals. Outdoor cats sometimes are stolen. They also may be hit by cars or attacked by other animals.

All cats mark their territories by leaving their scent on objects they scratch. Cats also scratch to release tension and keep their claws

Indoor Orientals need a scratching post.

sharp. Owners can train their cats to use scratching posts rather than scratch furniture, curtains, or carpet. Owners can buy a scratching post at a pet store or cat show or make one from wood and carpet.

Owners who keep their Orientals indoors must provide a litter box. These boxes are filled with small bits of clay or other material. Cats eliminate waste in litter boxes.

Cats may refuse to use a dirty litter box. Owners should clean the waste out of the box each day. They should change the litter at least once each week.

Feeding

Like all cats, Orientals need high-quality food to stay healthy and strong. Most cat foods sold in supermarkets or pet stores provide a balanced, healthy diet for Orientals.

Owners can choose from several kinds of cat food for their Orientals. Some owners feed their cats dry food. This food usually is less expensive than other types of food. Dry food can help keep cats' teeth clean. It does not spoil if it is left in a dish.

Some owners feed their Orientals moist, canned food.

Other owners feed their Orientals moist, canned food. This type of food can quickly spoil. It should not be left out for more than one hour.

The amount of food needed depends on the cat's size and appetite. Owners who feed their cats moist food usually feed adult cats twice each day. They feed kittens four times each day. Breeders and veterinarians can help

Owners should comb their Oriental Longhairs' fur each day with a metal comb.

owners decide how much food their cats need each day.

Cats need to drink plenty of water each day to stay healthy. Owners should make sure their Orientals always have clean water. Owners should change the water and wash the water dish once each day.

Food and water bowls should be glass or stainless steel. Germs are more likely to grow on plastic bowls.

Grooming

Oriental Shorthairs need little grooming. Owners should brush their Oriental Shorthairs at least once each week with a soft bristle brush. They then can wipe the cat's coat with their hands or a soft cloth called a chamois. This cloth helps keep the cat's coat smooth and shiny.

Oriental Longhairs need more grooming than Oriental Shorthairs do. Owners should comb their Oriental Longhairs' fur each day with a metal comb.

Cats' fur sometimes clumps together in mats. Mats are more common in longhaired cats such as the Oriental Longhair. Owners should never cut out mats with scissors. This dangerous practice can injure the cat's skin and damage its fur. Instead, a veterinarian or groomer can remove mats with a special tool. Groomers are people trained to bathe, brush, comb, and clip pets.

Long hairs grow in most cats' ears. Some owners clip these hairs from their Orientals' ears when they exhibit the cats in shows. Veterinarians or groomers can show owners how to properly clip the cats' ear hairs.

Nail Care

The tip of a cat's claw is called the nail. Orientals should have their nails trimmed about once each week. Cats with trimmed nails are less likely to damage carpet or furniture. Their nails are also less likely to become ingrown. Ingrown nails can occur when a cat does not sharpen its claws often. The claws then grow into the pad or bottom of the paw. This growth can cause serious, painful infections.

Owners should begin trimming their Orientals' nails when the cats are very young. Kittens then become used to having their nails trimmed as they grow older. Veterinarians or groomers can show owners how to trim their Orientals' nails with a special nail clipper.

Dental Care

All cats need regular dental care to protect their teeth and gums from plaque. This coating of bacteria and saliva causes tooth decay and gum disease. Dry cat food helps remove plaque from Orientals' teeth. Owners also should brush their cats' teeth at least once each week. They can use a toothbrush made for cats

Owners should trim their Orientals' nails about once each week.

or a soft cloth. Owners should use a toothpaste made for cats when brushing their Orientals' teeth. Toothpaste made for people can make cats sick.

Regular brushing may not be enough to remove the plaque from older Oriental cats' teeth. A veterinarian can clean these cats' teeth once each year.

Oriental Longhairs may be more likely to have hairballs than Oriental Shorthairs are.

Health Problems

Oriental cats have few health problems. Like all cats, they may get a condition called chin acne. Crusty black patches form on the cat's chin. Both food allergies and plastic food bowls can cause chin acne. Owners can help prevent chin acne by putting their Orientals' food and water in stainless steel or glass bowls.

Orientals sometimes get hairballs. This condition is more common in Oriental

Longhairs. Cats swallow loose pieces of fur as they groom their coats. This fur can form a ball in the cat's stomach. The cat then vomits the hairball. Large hairballs sometimes can block the cat's digestive system. Cats with this condition may need surgery.

Regular brushing is the best way to prevent hairballs. This practice removes loose fur before the cat can swallow it. Owners also can give their Orientals medicines to prevent hairballs. These medicines contain petroleum jelly. The jelly coats the hairballs in the cat's stomach and helps them pass harmlessly in the cat's waste.

Veterinarian Visits

Oriental cats should visit a veterinarian at least once each year. Older cats may need to visit a veterinarian more often. Older cats may have more health problems than younger cats. More frequent checkups can help veterinarians find and treat these problems.

A person who buys or adopts an Oriental should take it to a veterinarian for a checkup as soon as possible. The veterinarian will check the cat's heart, lungs, and other organs.

The veterinarian also will check the cat's eyes, ears, mouth, and coat.

The veterinarian will give vaccinations to the Oriental. Vaccinations are shots of medicine that help prevent diseases such as rabies. This deadly disease is spread by animal bites. Both people and animals can die from rabies. Most states and provinces have laws requiring pets to be vaccinated against rabies.

Veterinarians also can vaccinate cats for other diseases such as upper respiratory infections. These diseases can cause breathing problems, fever, and death.

Orientals should receive some vaccinations each year. They should receive others less often. Owners and veterinarians should keep a record of the vaccination dates. This record helps owners make sure their Orientals have received all the needed vaccinations.

Veterinarians also spay and neuter cats. These surgeries remove the cat's reproductive organs. The cats then cannot breed.

Owners who are not planning to breed their cats should have them spayed or neutered. These surgeries keep unwanted kittens from being born. They also keep cats healthy by

The sleek Oriental cat can be a friendly, active family pet.

helping prevent diseases such as infections and cancers of the reproductive organs. Spayed and neutered cats usually have calmer personalities than cats that are not spayed or neutered.

People who bring an Oriental into their home can look forward to a friendly, active companion. The sleek, curious Oriental will provide its owner with many years of affection and entertainment.

Pointed ears

Wedge-shaped head

ORIENTAL SHORTHAIR

Tube-shaped body

Whiplike tail

Long legs

Quick Facts about Cats

A male cat is called a tom. A female cat is called a queen. A young cat is called a kitten. A family of kittens born at one time is called a litter.

Origin: Shorthaired cat breeds descended from a type of African wildcat called *Felis lybica*. Longhaired breeds may have descended from Asian wildcats. People domesticated or tamed these breeds as early as 1500 B.C.

Types: The Cat Fanciers' Association accepts 40 domestic cat breeds for competition. The smallest breeds weigh about 5 to 7 pounds (2.3 to 3.2 kilograms) when grown. The largest breeds can weigh more than 18 pounds (8.2 kilograms). Cat breeds may be either shorthaired or longhaired. Cats' coats can be a variety of colors. These colors include many shades of white, black, gray, brown, and red.

Reproduction: Most cats are sexually mature at 5 or 6 months. A sexually mature female cat goes into estrus several times each year. Estrus also is called "heat." During this time, she can mate with a male. Kittens are born about 65 days after breeding. An average litter includes four kittens.

Development: Kittens are born blind and deaf. Their eyes open about 10 days after birth. Their hearing develops at the same time. They can live on their own when they are 6 weeks old.

Life span: With good care, cats can live 15 or more years.

Sight: A cat's eyesight is adapted for hunting. Cats are good judges of distance. They see movement more easily than detail. Cats also have excellent night vision.

Hearing: Cats can hear sounds that are too high for humans to hear. A cat can turn its ears to focus on different sounds.

Smell: A cat has an excellent sense of smell. Cats use scents to establish their territories. Cats scratch or rub the sides of their faces against objects. These actions release a scent from glands between their toes or in their skin.

Taste: Cats cannot taste as many foods as people can. For example, cats are not very sensitive to sweet tastes.

Touch: Cats' whiskers are sensitive to touch. Cats use their whiskers to touch objects and sense changes in their surroundings.

Balance: Cats have an excellent sense of balance. They use their tails to help keep their balance. Cats can walk on narrow objects without falling. They usually can right themselves and land on their feet during falls from short distances.

Communication: Cats use many sounds to communicate with people and other animals. They may meow when hungry or hiss when afraid. Cats also purr. Scientists do not know exactly what causes cats to make this sound. Cats often purr when they are relaxed. But they also may purr when they are sick or in pain.

Words to Know

chin acne (CHIN AK-nee)—a skin condition that can be caused by food allergies or plastic food and water bowls

estrus (ESS-truss)—a physical state of a female cat during which she will mate with a male cat; estrus also is known as "heat."

euthanize (YOO-thuh-nize)—to put an animal to death by injecting it with a substance that stops its breathing or heartbeat

neuter (NOO-tur)—to remove a male animal's testicles so it cannot reproduce

spay (SPAY)—to remove a female animal's uterus and ovaries so it cannot reproduce

tortoiseshell (TOR-tuh-shell)—a cat that has a mixture of red and black fur

vaccination (vak-suh-NAY-shun)—a shot of medicine that protects a person or animal from disease

veterinarian (vet-ur-uh-NER-ee-uhn)—a doctor who is trained to treat the illnesses and injuries of animals

To Learn More

Alderton, David. *Cats.* New York: DK
Publishing, 2000.

Fogle, Bruce. *The New Encyclopedia of the
Cat.* New York: DK Publishing, 2001.

Mattern, Joanne. *The Siamese Cat.* Learning
about Cats. Mankato, Minn.: Capstone
High-Interest Books, 2001.

Miller, Lynn. *The Guide to Owning an
Oriental Shorthair Cat.* Neptune City, N.J.:
T.F.H. Publications, 2000.

You can read articles about Orientals in
Cat Fancy magazine.

Useful Addresses

American Cat Fanciers Association (ACFA)
P.O. Box 1949
Nixa, MO 65714-1949

Canadian Cat Association (CCA)
289 Rutherford Road South
Unit 18
Brampton, ON L6W 3R9
Canada

Cat Fanciers' Association (CFA)
P.O. Box 1005
Manasquan, NJ 08736-0805

The International Cat Association (TICA)
P.O. Box 2684
Harlingen, TX 78551

Oriental Shorthairs of America
P.O. Box 821
West Windsor, NJ 08550

Internet Sites

American Cat Fanciers Association
http://www.acfacat.com

Canadian Cat Association
http://www.cca-afc.com

Cat Fanciers' Association
http://www.cfainc.org

The International Cat Association (TICA)
http://www.tica.org

Oriental Shorthairs of America
http://www.geocities.com/heartland/woods/
4291

**Pet Net's Cat Pages—Oriental Shorthair
Online Cat Breed Resource**
http://www.pet-net.net/oriental.htm

Index